# What Is the Story of Romeo and Juliet?

by Max Bisantz

illustrated by

Penguin W

Dedicated to theater artists and magic makers.
For Anthony—MB

For Natalie, she is the sun—DM

PENGUIN WORKSHOP
An imprint of Penguin Random House LLC, New York

First published in the United States of America by Penguin Workshop,
an imprint of Penguin Random House LLC, New York, 2023

Visit us online at penguinrandomhouse.com.

Library of Congress Control Number: 2023023597

Printed in the United States of America

ISBN 9781524792244 (paperback)          10 9 8 7 6 5 4 3 2 1 WOR
ISBN 9781524792251 (library binding)     10 9 8 7 6 5 4 3 2 1 WOR

# Contents

Sir Elton John

# What Is the Story of Romeo and Juliet?

When the biggest stars from Walt Disney Studios arrived in Hollywood for the premiere of a new animated movie, celebrities including Zendaya, James McAvoy, and Sir Elton John walked on a fuzzy blue carpet toward the doors of the El Capitan Theatre.

Inside, the audience sat in green chairs and marveled at the shiny gold ceiling. Suddenly, the lights dimmed. *Gnomeo & Juliet* in 3D was starting. The audience watched a small animated garden gnome appear on-screen.

"The story you are about to see has been told before," the gnome said. "A lot."

Everyone in the theater giggled. They knew the exact story the gnome was talking about. The movie continued, and two gnomes named

Gnomeo and Juliet lit up the screen. They met. They fell in love. They picked flowers. There was only one problem: Juliet's family lived on one side of the garden fence, and Gnomeo's family lived on the other. Those two families did not get along.

Laughter filled the theater as gnomes and flamingos danced across the screen. The crowd gasped when gnomes fought one another with lawn mowers. Luckily, the movie had a happy ending: Gnomeo and Juliet's love proved too strong for their family's disapproval.

When the movie ended, the crowd rose to their feet. "Bravo!" they cheered, as the movie's creators bowed.

It's difficult to believe that *Gnomeo & Juliet* is based on a tragic love story that is over five hundred years old! The first gnome to appear in the movie even hinted about that. That story is called Romeo and Juliet.

4

There have been many love stories written over time in all parts of the world. None are as famous as the story of Romeo and Juliet.

Movie audience applauds *Gnomeo & Juliet*

# CHAPTER 1
## Young Love

William Shakespeare was born in April of 1564, in Stratford-upon-Avon, England. Like other babies in this time and place, little William was probably given a taste of honey and butter right after he was born, followed by a healthy serving of jellied hare's brains for strength. (A hare is a mammal that resembles a large rabbit.) On April 26, the infant Shakespeare was then carried down to the nearby church to be baptized into the Christian faith. In

Shakespeare's time, nearly 20 percent of babies didn't live past their first month. Shakespeare's father, John, and his mother, Mary, had already lost two daughters before William was born. They did everything they could to make sure young William would grow up healthy and strong.

William did survive, and he grew into a strong young boy. He lived with his parents, brothers, and sisters in a wooden house on a busy street in town. John ran a glove-making shop from the front of their home. Making gloves was an important business in sixteenth-century England.

# To Make a Glove

For centuries, gloves have been used for practical reasons like warmth and protection and for athletic sports like boxing.

In the 1300s, women began wearing gloves purely for fashion. These gloves were made out of expensive fabrics like lace and linen. Gloves became so popular that in 1349, glove makers in London formed a guild, their own group of artisans. They called themselves the Worshipful Company of Glovers of London.

After Queen Elizabeth I took the throne in 1558, fashionable gloves reached an all-time high. Men and women wore gloves covered in jewels and sprayed with perfume to show their status. In 1638, the Worshipful Company of Glovers of London received a royal charter from the king. The guild exists to this day. Their motto is: "True Hearts and Warm Hands."

As a boy, William liked to escape the noise of town and explore the countryside with his brothers and sisters. Right outside of Stratford, lush meadows and pastures, sheep farms, and

trails were the perfect places for William and his siblings to explore. They spent hours roaming the forest and learning about all the plants, weeds, and flowers that sprouted from the ground.

Safety was always a concern, even in the woods. Drifters and local outlaws sometimes hid among the trees to avoid capture by local authorities. William and his siblings made sure to stay clear of dangerous people while they roamed the countryside. But that didn't stop the children from exploring! One of their favorite places to visit was an old bone house, or crypt, built in the back of a church. The crypt stored the remains of the town's dead. At the time, the bubonic (say: boo-BAH-nick) plague was sweeping through Europe. One out of every ten people in Stratford died. Although William and his siblings couldn't see inside the building, they would sneak around the outside of the crypt and imagine what horrors lay just inside its four walls. They'd scare one another silly with made-up stories about the dead people who were buried there.

As he got older, William started attending school six days a week at the King Edward VI

School in his hometown. School was very strict when Shakespeare was a student. The school day started at around six or seven in the morning with daily prayers. Next, students attended classes in Latin, math, or ancient Greek. A breakfast of bread and ale was served at nine, followed by more classes. The children then returned home around one for dinner with their families. They came back to school for more classes until five at night. William and his classmates only had about fifteen minutes each day for recess!

King Edward VI School

# The Bubonic Plague

The bubonic plague is a disease that is spread through the bites of infected fleas. When people are bitten, the disease is passed onto humans. Symptoms include fever, nausea, and large bumps on the body called "buboes." Without treatment, symptoms get worse and lead to chills, muscle cramps, and death.

The first known pandemic of bubonic plague occurred in the Roman Empire around AD 541. It is believed that twenty-five to a hundred million people died at that time.

Plague doctor mask from the 1600s

The second pandemic was called the Black Death. It began in Mongolia and Central Asia in the 1300s. From there, it spread to Western Europe and continued to cycle around the continent for two hundred years. Governments throughout Europe closed public places like theaters, baths, and markets to try to stop the spread of the disease. Around twenty-five million people, or a third of all Europeans, died in this plague.

Another pandemic of bubonic plague spread from China around the world in 1894. Over fifteen million people, mostly in China and India, died from the disease.

Today, doctors have a cure for bubonic plague. Antibiotics, used widely for the first time in the 1920s, can stop the disease in its tracks. People all over the world, including the United States, still catch the bubonic plague. Luckily, there is now a cure, and the disease typically goes away with medical treatment.

William was a very good student. As the years went by, he excelled in arts and in poetry. But school was too strict for someone like William, and he soon found other hobbies and interests. In fact, he had a big secret.

William was in love. The object of his affection was a young woman named Anne Hathaway. Anne was the beautiful daughter of a wealthy farmer. She was older than William and took her work on the farm seriously. William couldn't contain his feelings for Anne any longer. He told Anne that he loved her, and she revealed that she loved him back. They hoped to be married.

Anne Hathaway

There was one problem: William was only eighteen, and in England, he was still too young to get married without his father's permission. John Shakespeare could be a difficult man. Instead, William and Anne fled Stratford to a nearby town, to be married in secret. Anne's friends Fulk Sandells and John Richardson stood in for their parents and gave permission for William to marry Anne.

Despite the rocky start, some historians believe that William and Anne moved back in with William's family shortly after their marriage.

Anne and William had three children together: Susanna was the oldest, followed by twins, Hamnet and Judith. William likely worked as a lawyer's clerk to provide for his family in his small childhood home. But William had big dreams.

He wanted to move to London, England's capital city. Queen Elizabeth I was England's ruler. The Renaissance (say: REH-nuh-SAHNS), a period of artistic and cultural exploration that had started in Italy, had finally made its way to England. New ideas about music, literature, and painting were taking root in London. Artists were respected and able to earn a good salary.

One of the most famous paintings of the Renaissance, *Mona Lisa* by Leonardo da Vinci

# Queen Elizabeth I of England (1533–1603)

Elizabeth was the daughter of King Henry VIII and his second wife, Anne Boleyn. When Elizabeth was two years old, her mother was executed. While her half-siblings ruled England, Elizabeth was imprisoned  or placed under house arrest for much of her young life.

After the death of her half-sister, Mary Tudor, Elizabeth was released from prison. She became the queen of England at age twenty-five. Due to her many years of private schooling, she was one of the most educated people to ever rule England. Under her reign, arts and sciences were celebrated, in what is now known as the Elizabethan era.

William had always loved writing and was often praised for his poetry. He decided to move alone to London to pursue a career in the theater. There, he hoped to make a name for himself and bring honor and fortune to the Shakespeare family name.

In London, William found work with an acting troupe called the Lord Chamberlain's Men. He performed in plays all over the city. William also began writing many of the plays that the actors performed. Most were historical plays about kings and queens. One was a comedy about mistaken twins. But there was another kind of story that he wanted to write.

William hoped to write the best love story of all time. He was lonely in London without his family. William would visit Stratford when he could, but he was much older now. He was no longer a school-age boy madly in love with a beautiful young farm girl. He wanted to write a story about young love, the kind he had felt in his youth. But this wouldn't be an ordinary love story. His love story would include fierce sword fights and mysterious potions. There would be kissing. This story would prove that love conquers hate. And William already had his inspiration.

## CHAPTER 2
## Mariotto and Gianozza

In William Shakespeare's time, it was common to take a well-known story and change it in small ways to make it seem new. Most people back then could not read or write. Seeing plays or listening to storytellers was often the only way they were entertained. If the audience knew the ending, they would still come to the theater to see their favorite tales told in a different way.

Some of Shakespeare's plays sprang from his own imagination, but many of them were adapted from other writers. One of his favorite love stories, *The Tragicall Historye of Romeus and Iuliet,*

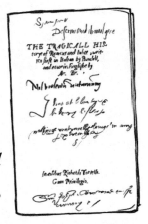

was set in Italy and featured two people in love who were from two families that did not get along. William probably read a version of this story translated from Italian by a poet named Arthur Brooke. But this love story existed long before Shakespeare and Brooke were even born.

In the 1400s, an Italian poet named Masuccio Salernitano wrote a story called "Mariotto and Gianozza." The story was set in Siena, Italy, and featured two teenagers who were in love. Gianozza is from a noble family. She loves Mariotto but knows her father will never approve of their marriage. Mariotto and Gianozza rush to a friar, a religious man similar to a monk, and marry in secret. Then Mariotto gets into a fight with a neighbor and accidentally

Masuccio Salernitano

kills him. He is ordered to leave Siena and flees to Egypt to live in his uncle's house.

Gianozza's father demands that she marry a wealthy man who he has chosen for her. Instead, she comes up with a plan. Gianozza asks the friar who married them to give her a special potion that will make her appear dead for just one day before reawakening. Gianozza drinks the potion.

Her family believes she's dead and buries her in the family crypt. When Gianozza awakes, she secretly escapes to Egypt to be reunited with Mariotto.

There's just one problem: Mariotto never learns of Gianozza's plan. Instead, he only hears that Gianozza is believed to be dead. Mariotto is so devastated that he returns to Siena to be by her grave. Once there, he is discovered and put to death for the murder of his neighbor.

Gianozza arrives in Egypt and learns of her beloved husband's death. In mourning, she returns to Siena, where her family moves her into a convent—a community of religious women called nuns. While there, she dies of sadness, mourning for her lost love.

The story of Mariotto and Gianozza was very popular during its time. Writers all over Europe retold the story in their own ways, adding characters and changing the plot.

By the time William Shakespeare read *The Tragicall Historye of Romeus and Iuliet*, the names had already been changed from the original and the story was over one hundred years old! People were familiar with it. Shakespeare knew that his version of the story would have to be better than the others. He wanted to write a play that would be remembered forever.

# CHAPTER 3
## The Play's the Thing

Shakespeare sat down and began to write his new play, called simply *Romeo and Juliet*. The play is written in five acts, which means five sections of the story, each with different scenes or locations. It begins with a single actor onstage. The actor tells the audience what to expect.

Verona •

• Siena

Italy

• Rome

"Two households, both alike in dignity," says the actor, "in fair Verona, where we lay our scene." The play is about two families from Verona, Italy, who are both of the same class, or stature ("alike in dignity"). The actor tells us that two "star-crossed" lovers will meet a sad end. *Star-crossed* means that Romeo and Juliet's destiny is written in the stars, and that whatever happens in the story, it will not have a happy ending.

The setting of the play then moves to the town square. The two families, the Montagues and the Capulets, break into a sword fight in the middle of the day. The prince of Verona—the head of their town—breaks up the fight and sets the death penalty for any more fighting between the two families.

Meanwhile, Juliet's father, Lord Capulet, has agreed to let a handsome man named Count Paris marry his beautiful daughter—if she agrees. He invites the count to a party that evening with Juliet. But Juliet is not sure if she is ready to get married. Her nurse, one of the Capulets' loyal servants, encourages her to consider the count's offer.

When we are introduced to the character of Romeo, he is in love with a woman named Rosaline. His cousin Benvolio and their friend

Mercutio decide to take Romeo to a masquerade (say: MAS-keh-RAYD) ball at the Capulet house to take his mind off Rosaline. A masquerade ball is a grand event where guests "disguise" themselves in fashionable masks, fine clothes, wigs, and jewels. Guests spend the night dancing to live music and enjoying rich food and drinks. Romeo and Benvolio are not invited to the party: They are Montagues, enemies of the Capulets. But wearing masks, they'll never get caught!

# Shakespeare Speak

Shakespeare used many different forms of poetry in his plays. Characters speak in different rhythms and rhymes depending on social status, age, and character traits.

*Iambic pentameter* (say: eye-AM-bik pen-TAM-eh-ter) is a meter in poetry that has ten syllables to each line.

Juliet says, "The / clock / struck / nine / when / I / did / send / the / nurse.

In / half / an / hour / she / pro / mised / to / re / turn." Her manner of speaking (using ten syllables in each line) shows that she is upper-class and the hero of the play.

The nurse speaks in *blank verse*. This type of poetic meter has no rhythm or set number of syllables, and sounds like common speech. The nurse says, "Well, you have made a simple choice.

Nurse

You know not how to choose a man. Romeo? No, not he." This blunt way of talking shows that she is from a lower class and is there to provide humor to the story.

At the ball, Romeo, still wearing his mask, meets Juliet. The two share a kiss and quickly fall in love. Later that evening, they discover the truth about each other: Juliet is a Capulet, and Romeo is a Montague. They are from rival families.

Later that night, Romeo sneaks over the Capulets' garden wall to visit Juliet. Suddenly, Juliet walks onto the balcony off her bedroom, right above Romeo.

"But soft! What light through yonder window breaks?" Romeo says. "It is the east, and Juliet is the sun." He thinks Juliet is more beautiful than the sun.

Juliet looks out into the night and begins to speak, not knowing that Romeo is in her garden.

"O Romeo, Romeo! Wherefore art thou Romeo?" she asks. "Deny thy father and refuse thy name." She wishes Romeo had a different name, because her family is against Romeo.

"What's in a name?" she wonders. "That which we call a rose by any other name would smell as sweet."

After hearing these words, Romeo rises and speaks. He agrees with Juliet.

"My name, dear saint, is hateful to myself," he says.

It is love, Romeo declares, that has brought him to Juliet's garden. But she worries for his safety.

"If they do see thee, they will murder thee," Juliet warns.

But love is too strong for them to keep apart. The two teenagers agree to make a plan tomorrow to marry in secret. After knowing each other for only one brief evening, they feel ready to spend their lives together.

"Good night, good night! Parting is such sweet sorrow," Juliet tells her love.

The next day, the nurse helps the young couple sneak away to be married in secret by Friar Laurence.

Friar Laurence

The next scene begins with a violent onstage fight. It is morning in Verona, and the men of the Capulet and Montague families find themselves facing off in the town square. Juliet's cousin Tybalt is furious that the Montague men sneaked into the ball. Romeo enters, and Tybalt challenges him to a duel.

"Thou art a villain!" says Tybalt.

Tybalt

Mercutio

Romeo refuses to fight, but Mercutio draws his sword.

"Tybalt, you rat-catcher," Mercutio challenges.

The Capulets and the Montagues fight. Tybalt
kills Romeo's best friend, Mercutio. In a fit of
rage, Romeo fights back and stabs Juliet's cousin
to death. Benvolio tells Romeo to run. If the
prince catches him, he will be killed. Romeo flees

the scene and goes to Friar Laurence, who hides him.

When the prince of Verona arrives, Benvolio explains what happened and defends Romeo's honor. The prince agrees to save Romeo from

death. Instead, he banishes him to life in exile. He can never come back to Verona.

The nurse shares the terrible news with Juliet: Romeo has killed Tybalt and will be exiled. Juliet is devastated. Romeo comes to Juliet's room to say goodbye, and then leaves for the nearby town of Mantua. Juliet's mother, Lady Capulet, arrives to tell Juliet that she must marry Count Paris at once. Juliet pleads with her mother to delay the marriage. Her mother refuses.

"Fie, fie, what, are you mad?" her mother cries.

Juliet flees to Friar Laurence for advice. She would rather die than marry Count Paris! Friar Laurence has a secret potion that will solve all of Juliet's problems. This potion will make Juliet appear dead for twenty-four hours. Then her wedding to Count Paris will be called off, and Juliet's body will be taken to the family crypt. Once she's alone, the potion will wear off, and Juliet will awaken.

Lady Capulet

Then, she can escape the crypt and be with Romeo. Friar Laurence promises he'll send a messenger to tell Romeo the plan.

That night, alone in her bedroom, Juliet faces her fear and drinks the potion. She'll do anything to be reunited with Romeo.

"Romeo, I come! This do I drink to thee," she says. She falls into a deep sleep. The next morning, the Capulet family awakens to find Juliet's body cold and stiff. They mourn her death and bring her to the family crypt, as she planned.

But Romeo never learns about the plan. The letter Friar Laurence sent hasn't reached Mantua. Due to an outbreak of the plague, the messenger was not allowed to leave Verona. Instead, Romeo hears news from his servant, Balthasar, that his wife is dead. Romeo is heartbroken. He goes to an apothecary—a person who makes and sells medicine and herbal remedies—and buys a potion that will end his life. Then he travels back to Verona to see his beloved Juliet one last time and to die in her arms.

Romeo sneaks into the Capulet family crypt, but not before running into Count Paris in the cemetery. They duel, and Romeo kills the count! He then enters the crypt to find Juliet under the potion's spell. Romeo believes her to be dead. He crawls into her arms and pledges to end his life to be united with her in death.

"Here's to my love!" he shouts before he drinks the potion and dies.

# Potions and Poisons

Many of Shakespeare's plays, including *Romeo and Juliet*, feature herbal potions and poisons that were mostly based on real plants found in nature. They were capable of healing, helping people sleep, or even killing an enemy.

- Juliet's sleeping potion is believed to be made from deadly nightshade, a plant that grows wild in Europe.

Deadly nightshade

- Romeo drinks a fast-acting potion that brings a quick death. Scientists believe this poison to be cyanide, which is made using animal horns or leather.

- Shakespeare's play *A Midsummer Night's Dream* features a love potion made from a wild pansy.
- King Hamlet in the play *Hamlet* is killed by a poison liquid dropped into his ear. This poison is believed to be a deadly plant called henbane that grows in Southern Europe and India.

At that moment, Juliet awakes from her spell. She looks around to find her husband dead with an empty bottle of potion. She knows what Romeo has just done.

"I will kiss thy lips; Haply some poison yet doth hang on them," she says.

She is hoping to absorb some of the deadly poison from his lips, but it doesn't work. Juliet can't imagine living in a world without her Romeo. She looks around and picks up his dagger.

A few moments later, both Romeo and Juliet are found dead in the crypt. Word spreads around town, and their parents enter the tomb to see their children for the last time. The grieving parents agree that their fighting must come to an end. They have lost too much. They make a bond of peace.

Lord Capulet and Lord Montague

"O brother Montague, give me thy hand," Lord Capulet says.

At the very end of the play, after the warring families have made peace, the prince of Verona says sadly, "For never was a story of more woe, Than this of Juliet and her Romeo."

# CHAPTER 4
# Pig's Blood and Nutshells

No one knows for sure the exact date of the first production of Shakespeare's *Romeo and Juliet*. But scholars know what it looked like and where it took place. In 1592, as the bubonic plague swept through Europe, thousands of citizens were dying in the street. To stop the disease from spreading in London, the mayor shut down all theaters and public meeting places. Actors moved all performances to theaters outside the city limits.

These playhouses (another word for theaters) were large wooden structures two or three stories high, without roofs. All the seats looked onto a courtyard where the actors performed. Members of the upper classes sat in the top seats with the best views. Commoners, ordinary people without family titles, paid pennies to stand on the ground level. These people were called "the groundlings." They would eat hazelnuts, throw shells, laugh, cry, and shout at the actors.

On opening night in 1597, hundreds of people fled the city of London to the outskirts of town to see the play. The opening fight scene of act one in *Romeo and Juliet* stunned the crowds. Actors at the time were trained in stage combat, the art of making fight scenes look real. The Capulets and the Montagues swung swords and jabbed daggers just inches from the actors.

Later in the play, it was the Capulet family's

turn to take the stage. All the members of the Capulet family, even Juliet, were played by men. In Shakespeare's time, it was against the law for women to appear onstage. Young boys and smaller men dressed in women's clothes to play the female roles.

The first person to play Juliet onstage was likely a boy actor named Robert Goffe. Robert was one of the best boy actors in the Lord Chamberlain's Men. He became famous for portraying female characters.

Richard Burbage was probably the first man to play Romeo. He was a beloved actor at the time and a crowd favorite. For the famous balcony scene, Richard played Romeo standing on the stage while Robert Goffe, as Juliet, appeared above him on the stage's second level. Because the roof of the theater was open to the sky, when Romeo swore his love to the moon, the audience could look into the heavens with him.

# Boy Players

Before 1660 in England, it was considered "improper" for women and girls to act on the stage because of strict religious rules imposed by the government. Instead, boys between the ages of eight and twelve, whose voices were still high, dressed up as women and played all the female parts. Boy actors (called players) began their training as apprentices. They would help make costumes, practice lines, and act in small parts. They also learned female "gestures" to act more ladylike onstage.

Boy actors were often just as popular as adult male actors. When King Charles II of England outlawed boy actors in the 1660s, many successfully switched to playing adult male roles onstage, including two of the most well-known actors, Alexander Cooke and Edward Kynaston.

After Romeo and Juliet are married, the audience finally got what they wanted: a bloody good fight scene! For act three, actors had sewn pig intestines filled with blood into their costumes. When Tybalt and Mercutio are stabbed, real blood flew into the audience. The groundlings in the front were completely splattered in pig's blood and guts.

As the sad tale of Romeo and Juliet unfolded,

the audience grew quiet. The actor at the beginning of the show had warned them that the story would end badly. But no one knew just how dreadful the ending would be. When Juliet dies at the end of the play, blood spattered everywhere as tears flowed from the audience. When the final lines of *Romeo and Juliet* were spoken, the crowd jumped to its feet in appreciation for Shakespeare's play.

# Richard Burbage (1567–1619)

Richard Burbage was an actor and theater owner in London during the "golden age" of Elizabethan drama. He began acting as a teenager with a troupe called the Admiral's Men. By 1600, he was working with Shakespeare's company, the Lord Chamberlain's Men, where he played many of Shakespeare's famous roles the first time they were staged. Richard was also a talented artist who painted theater sets and portraits of famous people. Burbage was considered one of the first celebrity actors in history.

# CHAPTER 5
## Women Take the Stage

Shakespeare wrote over twenty-five plays after *Romeo and Juliet*. His dramas, such as *Macbeth* and *Hamlet*, combined witchcraft and ghosts with bloody historical tales. His comedies, such as *Twelfth Night* and *A Midsummer Night's Dream*, told of fairy kingdoms, mistaken identities, and less-serious characters. But *Romeo and Juliet* remained one of his most popular plays and continued to appear in theaters around London for the rest of his life. Shakespeare and his acting troupe, the Lord Chamberlain's Men, built a new theater called the Globe. There, they performed Shakespeare's plays, including *Romeo and Juliet*, again and again.

# The Globe Theatre

The Globe Theatre was constructed on the banks of the River Thames in London. It was built using the wood of another theater that had recently been dismantled. The Globe was a round, open-air amphitheater that was three stories high and could hold over three thousand people. The ground floor of the theater was called "the pit."

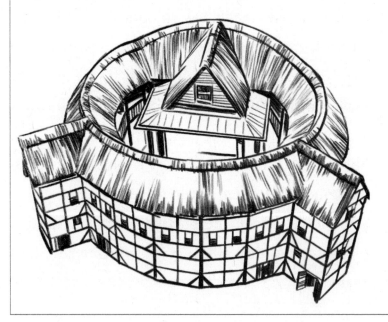

People paid a penny to stand in the pit and watch the performances. The more expensive seats occupied the second and third floors of the theater.

The actors performed on a wooden stage platform that extended from a wall to the center of the pit. The back wall of the stage had two doors separating the playing space from the actors' private quarters. Two columns supported a balcony where the musicians sat. Actors used the balcony to perform scenes like in *Romeo and Juliet*.

The Globe Theatre burned down in 1613 during a battle scene in one of Shakespeare's plays, *Henry VIII*. It was rebuilt the following year, only to be shut down and destroyed by the Puritan government in 1642, who believed the theater was "indecent."

In 1997, a modern reconstruction of the theater was built on the same plot of land as the original. The theater is an exact replica of the Globe Theatre and is called "Shakespeare's Globe."

Queen Elizabeth I invited the Lord Chamberlain's Men to perform a private show of *Romeo and Juliet* at her home, Greenwich Palace, downstream from London on the Thames.

Greenwich Palace

This time, there were no groundlings throwing nutshells. The queen enjoyed the show so much, the Lord Chamberlain's Men became a common sight at the royal court.

The play soon spread throughout Europe. From England, *Romeo and Juliet* first made its way to Germany. An acting company called *Englische Komödianten* translated the play from English into German. They performed for crowds all over the country, from small towns and villages to big cities like Dresden.

Back in England, William Shakespeare was a celebrity! Almost everyone had heard of his plays or seen them performed live. Some of Shakespeare's plays, including *Romeo and Juliet*, were even published and translated so people all around the world could read them. As Shakespeare got older, he continued to split his time between London for work and Stratford for family. He was a grandfather now! His oldest daughter, Susanna, had married and given birth to a daughter, Elizabeth. In 1616, at the age of fifty-two, Shakespeare died in his hometown of Stratford near his closest family and friends.

The grave of William Shakespeare

He was granted the honor of being buried in the Holy Trinity Church in Stratford.

Meanwhile, the country of England was in the middle of a big shake-up that changed life, and theater, forever. Queen Elizabeth I had died, and war erupted between England, Scotland, and Ireland. Control of the crown passed from ruler to ruler. One king was even beheaded.

Finally, a new king named Charles II took the throne. He brought peace to England, Scotland, and Ireland, and he made big changes across the region. One of those changes was allowing theaters to reopen.

King Charles II also allowed women to legally act in the theater. Women who had once been servants and farmhands suddenly became some of the most popular actors of the time. A young actor named Mary Saunderson is believed to be the first woman to play the role of Juliet. She was such a success that she became a big star on the British stage for the rest of her life.

King Charles II

# Mary Saunderson (1637–1712)

Mary Saunderson was born in England in 1637. As a young woman, she married a stage actor named Thomas Betterton. When King Charles II reopened public theaters and allowed women to act, Mary was one of the first to step onto the stage. Mary played Juliet, and her husband played Mercutio in the first production of *Romeo and Juliet* staged in over twenty years. This performance led to a successful career in the theater, and Mary began giving private acting lessons to young girls. King Charles II was so impressed by Mary that he asked her to tutor his nieces, the future queens of England, Anne and Mary.

# CHAPTER 6
## The Original Story

For another hundred years, many versions of the Romeo and Juliet story were performed onstage. And, as always, parts were changed over time. A British writer named Thomas Otway wrote a famous version. In his, Romeo and Juliet were renamed Marius and Lavinia. Thomas

Thomas Otway

gave the couple in his version a happy ending.

This happier version of the Romeo and Juliet story appeared on stages across Europe for nearly two hundred years. In the 1700s, a British actor and producer named David Garrick played Romeo in a sold-out production. In his version, Garrick removed any mention of Romeo's first love, Rosaline. He wanted the love between Romeo and Juliet to be even more pure.

David Garrick as Romeo

The story was so popular that by 1750, two of London's top theaters both ran the show at the same time. Audiences called this the "Battle of the Romeos."

In the 1750s, two brothers named William

and Lewis Hallam decided to bring the play to America. William, Lewis, twelve adult actors, and three child actors formed a theater group called the American Company. They sailed to Yorktown, Virginia, and performed Shakespeare's plays, including *Romeo and Juliet*. Then they traveled to New York, Philadelphia, and Jamaica.

Happier versions of Romeo and Juliet spread around the world. A Czech composer named Georg Benda wrote an opera called *Romeo und Julie* in 1776. The opera ended with Romeo's father and Juliet's father dancing together in joy.

By the 1800s, almost all of the sad parts had been removed from Shakespeare's story of Romeo and Juliet.

In 1845, two American sisters named Charlotte and Susan Cushman decided enough was enough. They loved the sad and tragic story of William Shakespeare's original *Romeo and Juliet*. They staged a version of the play where the actors spoke the exact words that Shakespeare had written. Susan played Juliet, and her older sister Charlotte played Romeo. The two women performed the original ending with the couple dying in each other's arms. Audiences were wowed. It had been over two hundred years since anyone had seen William Shakespeare's version of the play. They had forgotten how moving and how romantic it was. The show was such a success that it moved to London, where—just like the original had—it impressed the queen of England.

The Cushman sisters as Romeo and Juliet

"No one would ever have imagined she was a woman," Queen Victoria said of Charlotte's Romeo in 1845.

From that moment on, producers of the play stopped changing the words in *Romeo and Juliet*. In the end, Shakespeare was right. His play is now the best and official version of the story of Romeo and Juliet.

Queen Victoria

# CHAPTER 7
## Verona Goes to Hollywood

William Shakespeare's *Romeo and Juliet* continued to become even more famous over time. In the late 1800s, a man named George Crichton Miln formed a touring theater company and brought Shakespeare's play to Japan and Australia. Now it seemed the play had been performed in every corner of the world.

But by 1900, audiences had changed. Movie projectors had been invented, and more people were going to theaters to see movies, rather than plays and live stage performances. Silent films were the most popular form of entertainment. Audiences sat in darkened theaters and watched actors on-screen mouth the words of a script. Then, the actor's words, or dialogue, would appear on the screen to show what they had just said. Many directors created silent-film versions of *Romeo and Juliet*. These films were often successful.

A silent-film production of *Romeo and Juliet*

Then in 1927, a movie called *The Jazz Singer* opened. It was the first feature-length movie with sound. For the first time, audiences could hear actors on-screen speaking words.

In 1936, a director in Hollywood named Irving Thalberg wanted to make a movie version of *Romeo and Juliet* with sound. More people were seeing movies than plays. This would be the first time that movie audiences anywhere in the world could hear and see *Romeo and Juliet* on-screen. Irving cast his wife, Norma Shearer, as the young and beautiful Juliet. Historians worked hard to make the film set look like Verona, Italy. Costume designers worked for months to create clothes that looked like those from the 1500s, when *Romeo and Juliet* takes place. No detail was too small to overlook for Irving.

But one thing Irving didn't get right was the actors' ages. Norma Shearer was twenty years older than teenage Juliet. The actor who played Romeo, Leslie Howard, was over twenty-five years older than Romeo should have been!

Leslie Howard and Norma Shearer

The World is waiting for
NORMA SHEARER, LESLIE HOWARD
in "ROMEO AND JULIET".

Never in the history of Metro-Goldwyn
... there been so much interest
... during the

Opening night of *Romeo and Juliet* was a huge success. The movie earned a lot of money and was nominated for four Academy Awards. Today, it is considered one of the most important films of the 1930s.

# CHAPTER 8
# Broadway Magic

In the 1940s, a young choreographer named Jerome Robbins had an idea: He wanted to bring Romeo and Juliet to Broadway. But Jerome didn't want to stage Shakespeare's play. He wanted to create a new Broadway musical based on *Romeo and Juliet*. This time, the play would include music and dancing. It would be set in present-day New York City . . .

If anyone on Broadway could make this musical happen, it was Jerome Robbins. Jerome had been choreographing (directing dance movements) for Broadway musicals since the 1930s. One of his biggest musicals, *On the Town*, had been turned into a major Hollywood film starring the famous singer and actor Frank

Sinatra. To make a musical version of *Romeo and Juliet*, Robbins needed people to write the music and the story.

Jerome Robbins

Arthur Laurents

In 1947, Jerome asked the writer Arthur Laurents and composer Leonard Bernstein to work on the project. After working together for years, Arthur Laurents brought in a young songwriter, Stephen Sondheim, to help with the lyrics.

The four men changed the plot of *Romeo and Juliet* to reflect New York City in the 1950s. The character of Juliet became a young Puerto Rican woman named Maria. Romeo was now a young man named Tony of Irish and Polish descent.

The feuding families were represented as rival gangs called the Sharks and the Jets on the west side of Manhattan in New York City. At the time, there was real street violence every day between gangs of Puerto Rican immigrants and those of their Irish and Polish neighbors. The creators retitled the show *West Side Story*. This would be a true Romeo and Juliet story for the modern day.

Rehearsals for *West Side Story* were almost twice as long as any other Broadway show. There had never been so much dancing in a musical before. The music was loud and fast, like the energy of New York City. There was Latin salsa music for the Puerto Rican characters and songs that were slow and romantic for the young couple. The story was *mostly* based on Shakespeare's *Romeo and Juliet*, but in *West Side Story*, Juliet (now Maria) lives to tell her story.

# Stephen Sondheim (1930–2021)

Stephen Sondheim was born into a Jewish family in New York City. As a boy, he had a natural talent for music. He became friends with James Hammerstein, son of the famous Broadway lyricist Oscar Hammerstein. A lyricist is the person who writes the words to songs in musical theater. Oscar noticed Stephen's musical talent from an early age and mentored him to write for musical theater.

Stephen's first Broadway credit was when he wrote the lyrics to *West Side Story*, which opened in 1957. He was also a talented composer, and later musicals featured both his words and music. Stephen wrote original songs that combined traditional styles with modern ideas. Over his lifetime, Stephen received Tony Awards, the Pulitzer Prize, and a Grammy Award for musicals like *Sweeney Todd* and *Into the Woods*. Many consider Stephen to be among the most important and talented figures in American musical theater.

Broadway shows at the time had mostly all-white casts. This production of *West Side Story* featured actors of all different backgrounds: Puerto Rican, African American, Italian, Greek, and others. One of the most popular entertainers at the time, a Puerto Rican actress named Chita Rivera, played the role of Anita, Maria's best friend and confidante.

*West Side Story* opened on Broadway in 1957 to rave reviews. Audiences were stunned by the choreography, the music, and the tragedy of the two lovers. Much like the play *Romeo and Juliet* had changed drama on the stage, *West Side Story* is now considered to be the show that changed Broadway musicals forever.

# Puerto Ricans in
# the United States

Puerto Rico is an island commonwealth in the Atlantic Ocean around one thousand miles from the southern tip of Florida. The original inhabitants of Puerto Rico were the Taino people of the Caribbean. In the 1500s, the country of Spain conquered the island and the Taino people. Trade existed between Puerto Rico and the United States for centuries, and people moved between the two countries.

Then in 1898, the Spanish-American War broke out. People in Spanish-occupied Puerto Rico fled to the United States to seek refuge. Spain lost the war and gave the US government control of Puerto Rico. In 1917 President Woodrow Wilson signed the Jones-Shafroth Act, which gave Puerto Rican residents United States citizenship.

After the Great Depression and World War II, a large population of Puerto Ricans migrated to the United States to seek work. Many of them settled in New York City, forming neighborhoods, or "barrios," to continue the traditions of their homeland in their new communities. Today, over five million people of Puerto Rican descent live in the United States.

# CHAPTER 9
## And the Award Goes to . . .

*West Side Story* made the story of Romeo and Juliet more accessible than ever. The musical toured the United States. Then it opened in England in the West End, London's theater district. By 1960, producers wanted to make a movie version of *West Side Story*. They chose a director named Robert Wise who was known for creating gritty movies about New York City. They wanted to keep the musical as realistic as possible.

Robert Wise

*West Side Story*, the movie, opened on October 18, 1961. Crowds and critics raved. It was the most successful musical ever put on film. *West Side Story* won ten Academy Awards, including Best Supporting Actress for the young Puerto Rican actress Rita Moreno, who played Anita.

The movie musical brought even more attention to *West Side Story*. In the decades since it opened on Broadway and became an award-winning movie, over one hundred thousand performances of the musical have played in high schools, amateur theaters, and professional acting companies across the world. Much like the audiences in Shakespeare's time, modern audiences simply can't get enough of the story of two star-crossed teenagers and their forbidden love.

Rita Moreno as Anita

# Rita Moreno (1931–)

Rita Moreno was born Rosa Dolores Alverío Marcano in Humacao, Puerto Rico. She moved to New York City with her mother when she was a young girl. Rita landed her first role on Broadway when she was only thirteen. She appeared in films, including the blockbuster hit *Singin' in the Rain*.

When Rita won the Academy Award for Best Supporting Actress for her role as Anita in *West Side Story*, she was the first Puerto Rican actor to receive the award. She is one of the few performers to win all four major entertainment awards: an Emmy Award for television, a Grammy Award for music, an Academy Award (Oscar) for film, and a Tony Award for theater.

# CHAPTER 10
## All the World's a Stage

New adaptations of the story of Romeo and Juliet continue to be made to this day. In 1996, an Australian film director named Baz Luhrmann created another movie version of the story, called *Romeo + Juliet*. His film is set in the modern-day fictional city of Verona Beach. Everything in Baz's movie is modern. Characters drive cars, use guns instead of swords, and wear modern clothes. But Baz still wanted the actors to use the original Shakespearean language. Celebrity actors like Leonardo DiCaprio, Claire Danes, and Paul Rudd starred as Romeo, Juliet, and Count Paris.

In 2009, *West Side Story* returned to Broadway. This time, producers wanted to translate all the Puerto Rican songs and dialogue from English into Spanish. By 2010, Spanish was the most spoken language in the United States after English. Puerto Rican and Spanish-speaking actors would now be able to sing the songs of Maria, the character based on Juliet, in their native language.

Josefina Scaglione as Maria in the 2009 revival of *West Side Story*

For this production, Puerto Rican and native Spanish-speaking actors were not just in supporting roles. They played the leads. A Venezuelan actor named George Akram played Bernardo, Maria's cousin and the character based on Tybalt. An Argentinian actress named Josefina Scaglione played Maria, and an actress named Karen Olivo, of Puerto Rican and Dominican descent, played Anita.

Karen Olivo

When the revival of *West Side Story* opened on Broadway, Spanish- and English-language audiences flocked to the theater to watch the tragic love story unfold. The show was a huge success. The revival of *West Side Story* was nominated for four Tony Awards. Karen Olivo won a Tony for playing Anita. She dedicated her award to "everyone who has a dream."

Ten years later, Hollywood director Steven Spielberg decided to remake the film of *West Side Story* for a new generation of film audiences. With streaming services now available, people could watch the romantic story directly in their living rooms.

A cast of talented young performers including Rachel Zegler, Ansel Elgort, and Ariana DeBose played the major roles. Rita Moreno, in her late eighties, also appeared in the film as a neighborhood shopkeeper. Spielberg's *West Side Story* released in theaters on December 10, 2021.

Steven Spielberg (center) and the cast of *West Side Story* (2021) at its premiere

Again, Hollywood took notice. Spielberg's *West Side Story* was nominated for seven Academy Awards. Ariana DeBose, who played Anita, won an Academy Award for her work, becoming the first openly queer woman of color to receive the honor.

New generations of artists continue to put their own spins on Shakespeare's *Romeo and Juliet*. A new musical, *& Juliet* by Max Martin and David West Read, imagines a version of the play where Juliet survives. It opened in London's West End in 2019 and on Broadway in 2022.

References to Romeo and Juliet are all around us. Disney's *Gnomeo & Juliet* turned the love story into an animated comedy for young audiences in 2011. In *Toy Story 3*, the toys stage a full production of *Romeo and Juliet* with the hedgehog as Romeo and the little green alien as Juliet. The infamous "balcony scene" has been parodied in *The Simpsons*, commercials for Huggies diapers, and more. Taylor Swift's music video for "Love Story" mentions Juliet and features costumes and castles much like the play.

The story of the two families who do not get along, and their children who are caught in the middle of their quarrel, has been performed all over the world for nearly five hundred years. People like to be reminded that love conquers all, even if the story might end sadly. The tale of Romeo and Juliet is truly the best love story of all time.

# What's in a Name?

The story of Romeo and Juliet has inspired scientists, astronomers, and explorers for centuries. Many great discoveries have been named after the teenage couple.

- A pair of mountains in Vancouver, Canada, were named Mount Romeo and Mount Juliet in 1933. The mountains are separated by two rivers, which authorities named Montague and Capulet Creeks.

- In 1986, astronomers discovered a moon orbiting Uranus. They named the moon Juliet.

- Scientists named an endangered Sehuencas water frog Romeo in 2009, and later found and named another one Juliet in 2018. The frogs have reproduced and helped save their species.

# Bibliography

**\*Books for young readers**

Ackroyd, Peter. *Shakespeare: The Biography*. New York:
Random House, 2005.

\*Aliki. *William Shakespeare & the Globe*. New York:
Harper Collins, 1999.

Arnold, Catharine. *Globe: Life in Shakespeare's London*.
London: Simon & Schuster UK, 2015.

\*Asbury, Kelly, director. *Gnomeo & Juliet*. Walt Disney Studios,
2011.

Pritchard, R. E. *Shakespeare's England: Life in Elizabethan
& Jacobean Times*. Gloucestershire: Sutton Publishing
Limited, 1999.

Prunster, Nicole. *Romeo and Juliet before Shakespeare:
Four Early Stories of Star-Crossed Love*. Toronto:
CRSS Publications, 2000.

Wise, Robert, and Jerome Robbins, directors. *West Side Story*.
1961, United Artists.

# Timeline of Romeo and Ju

| 1476 | 1562 | 1564 | 1592 | 1597 | 1613 | 1616 | 1660 |

Arthur Brooke translates *The Tragicall Historye of Romeus and Iuliet* into English

All theaters in London close to protect against the plague

William Shakespeare dies at the age of fifty-two

"Mariotto and Gianozza" is published in Italy

*AN*
# EXCELLENT
conceited Tragedie
OF
Romeo and Iuliet.

As it hath been often (with great applaufe) plaid publiquely, by the right Honourable the L. of Hunsdon his Seruants.

LONDON,
Printed by Iohn Danter.
1597

Charles II permits women to act on the stage

Shakespeare's *Romeo and Juliet* is first performed

William Shakespeare is born in Stratford-upon-Avon, England

[The Globe Theatre, Bankside.]

The Globe Theatre burns down during a performance of Shakespeare's *Henry VIII*

| 1750 | 1845 | 1936 | 1957 | 1962 | 1996 | 2009 | 2021 |
|------|------|------|------|------|------|------|------|

The musical *West Side Story* opens on Broadway

Baz Luhrmann's film *Romeo + Juliet* opens

American sisters Charlotte and Susan Cushman perform *Romeo and Juliet* in its original Shakespearean language

A bilingual version of the musical *West Side Story* opens on Broadway

Rita Moreno wins an Academy Award for the 1961 movie musical version of *West Side Story*

*Romeo and Juliet*, a film starring Norma Shearer and Leslie Howard, opens in Hollywood

Steven Spielberg's film version of *West Side Story* opens

The "Battle of the Romeos" causes a frenzy in London